# BRAVING THE COCOON

*Inspirational Lessons*
*Learned by a Cancer Survivor*

By Jamie B. Medina

**TRILOGY**

*PROFESSIONAL PUBLISHING MEETS POWERFUL PROMOTION*

A wholly owned subsidary of **TBN**

# DEDICATION

This book is dedicated to my husband, Narciso.
You are the steadfast prayer warrior who tells me
I have power in Jesus' name and will not let me
wallow in self-pity. Thank you for your strength and
stubborn faith! Our family is blessed because of you.

# ACKNOWLEDGMENTS

I want to thank my Lord Jesus for being my all-sufficient one. You have been and continue to be everything I need.

Thank you to my beautiful children. You all are total blessings in my life. I'm so thankful for the joy you bring. I have no doubts that joy is good medicine to my bones.

Thank you to my husband, Narciso. You are tough and steadfast in prayer. I am so thankful you are my partner. We have grown up and learned so much together.

Thank you to my parents, Darvis and Phyllis. You are just all-around outstanding people whose love, generosity, hospitality, and patience have been beautiful examples of how to live life and treat people.

Thank you to my sister, Darla, and my brother, Phil. You took time out of your busy lives to come help take care of me. You are beautiful, amazing people.

Thank you to my dear sweet cousin Susan. Your exceptional kindness and willingness to share your Houston home with my family was a huge blessing to us in our most difficult time.  God bless you always!

Thank you, my church family (Victory Family Church). You all lift, encourage, and pray for me continually. I feel the strength of your prayers so many days.

Thank you to my school family (Wilson Elementary). You all encouraged me to write, and you demonstrated such amazing generosity to me.

I want to say a special thank you to the outstanding

doctors and nurses at MD Anderson Cancer Center in Houston, Texas. You are my definition of world peace. Thank you for working so tirelessly every day to eradicate the enemy of cancer.

# TABLE OF CONTENTS

# PREFACE

"What is mankind that you are mindful of them, human beings that you care for them?   You have made them a little lower than the angels, and crowned him with glory and honor. You made them rulers over the work of your hands; you put everything under their feet" (Psalm 8:4-6).

I have found myself wondering this same thing many times in the last few years. I guess I am in good company because the words above came from King David in the Bible. Why would God in all his infinite wisdom want to know me and to have me know Him? Why would He express His love to me? Why would He want to show me how to love and to live a great and beautiful life through the instructions in the Bible of the life His son Jesus lived? I have often considered myself lowly and unimportant, kind of like a worm or caterpillar in His eyes, but even the lowest of creatures have a job to do on this earth. If you are a worm, you make rich soil for things to grow. If you are a caterpillar, you are in a constant state of metamorphosis, which is a constant changing and growing phase of a beautiful butterfly or moth, which in turn becomes a pollinator to help things grow.

So I decided that if God is mindful of me, I must have an outrageously interesting job to do here in this world to point the way to His majestic love for us, and obviously, to help people grow. The verse above does state that we are "rulers over the works of His hands."

So with this being said at this moment, the job God

has set before me is to detail my exuberant account of the many lessons I have learned about His character and His love for me through the trials of cancer while pregnant, surgeries, treatments all while trying to care for my young family.

The fact is, I am not a preacher, pastor, or Bible scholar but have been "assigned" to tell you my story. This is not something I would willingly share in my own introverted mindset. Notice I put the word assigned in quotations because I believe strongly, as in the last ten years, I have had a joyful nagging feeling that will not let me get away from writing this account of His goodness to me, the works of His hands in my life.

Perhaps God is mindful because He created us with an enormous amount of potential, and He does not want a single bit of it wasted! Perhaps He created us to be the objects of His affection, to love us and us Him. Perhaps He is mindful of us because we reflect His glory and power in the unique talents He gives us all. That does not seem insignificant at all.

Sometimes to help us in our metamorphosis to understand why He is mindful, He allows us to experience adversity in our lives (trials) to develop certain skills, specifically total reliance on Him, which is necessary for our purpose, survival, or better yet, necessary to help love and encourage others to know and rely on His power.

As I embarked on serious reflection of my cancer experience as a young mom, I realized a big misconception. I was not insignificant. You see, that word means unimportant or hopeless. What I am is humble. That is something different and quite significant. Humble is lowly but powerful. Humble is an attitude of thankfulness. Humble says, "God, I cannot do anything without you!" Humble says, "I have no explanation for why I am here other than the power of God's almighty hand."

With that, I say, "I am thankful for the trial of cancer and treatment at such a tender time in my life." It was a time of metamorphosis that pushed me to see that God is so mindful of me. It was a time that has totally shaped the way I treat and love others and myself. It was a time when I learned so much about the character of God. My lessons are not just for me but for me to encourage others going through the most difficult trials. Rest assured, you are so precious and significant that the Mighty Creator is very mindful of you!

Heavenly Father,

I thank You for each silken thread of Your grace, mercy, and love. They squeeze about me so tightly to let me know You are with me. Each thread hanging on to me to show me that You who began a good work in me is sure to finish it! Please, Lord, let the threads You have put around my life be links to help those who read these words. Let us all become a clearer picture of Your image to this world. Take Your time on us in our cocoons. Speak softly to us so that we may be brave and courageous through each disappointment, trial, error, and heartbreak in our lives. Strip away anything that would hinder the beauty You see in us. Lord, let each amazing scar become a vein in the glorious wings that will help us fly to do Your works. Help us to fly high enough to see Your perspective on the life You give us. Let it be so in Jesus' precious name.

Amen!

# INTRODUCTION

A question was posed to me recently in my church life group, "Have you ever done anything bold by choice or by necessity? How did it bring You closer to Christ?" It did not take long for me to answer, "I went through cancer while I was pregnant with my fourth child." There was a small gasp. "Could you tell us about that?" our group leader asked… I had to think of what to say, and I just told the basic story and gave just a few examples of God's work through that experience. However, it did create a spark in me to finish writing this book which has been in the process for the last seven years.

You see, sometimes in our lives, God allows us to go through situations so perilous, adventurous, sometimes tragic, and sometimes so miraculous that it takes a while to process how God brought you through it. It also takes some deep reflection to see just exactly how He orchestrated every second of that time and kept His hand right on you through it all.

My journey through cancer was the way God got my attention by tangling me up in His cocoon, so to speak. With threads of trust, provision, hope, grace, comfort, joy, strength, and love, He wrapped me up so tight I could not do anything but marvel at His greatness. The only explanation I have for healing is that I serve a healing God who has amazing plans for me. He needed me to just be still and know He is God.

There is no doubt that God allowed me to go through

cancer for my own good. *He needed to work some things out in my character while He revealed His character as a loving, comforting, joyful, life-giving God: a most Heavenly Father.* My cancer experience lasted seven years. I came out stronger in character, more thankful and appreciative for the little things in life, and I do not sweat the small stuff.

I will never be the same person I was. Thank God. I still have some things to work on, but I am confident I was given this story to encourage others who may be going through similar situations, to restore hope where it may be fading, and to tell of His mighty works.

# 1

# UNASSUMING CATERPILLAR

A small self-sufficient caterpillar lives methodically, just crawling around, eating leaves, and never assuming life would be changing very soon.

Thirty-one years of crawling my way through life. I'm going to call myself the unassuming caterpillar: just trying to do things my own way, the best I had been taught. I was strong in my own mind and body. I could do everything on my own. I knew Jesus. I just did not want to bother Him! After all, there are people with much bigger problems than mine. So I continued to do everything with my own strength. Little did I know, I was not called to do everything on my own, and I was vulnerable.

At that time, my husband and I were getting back on track and pressing through a rocky spot in our marriage, trying to raise three children with the fourth one on the way. I was teaching special education full time, and he was working full time for our insurance company. Life seemed just fine and busy. As a family, we were starting to attend our church more regularly. We were getting stronger in our faith. We were starting to learn more about God's love for us, and all was moving along quite well.

Well, at least I thought. As I began to go through my fourth pregnancy, I was about seven months along, and I developed a black blister about the size of a quarter on my left calf. I did not think much about it other than it was ugly, and I covered it with a bandage most of the time.

My daughter, who was twelve and very observant, noticed it. (I'm going to say God made her notice it, just as He made her smart enough to think about it and mention it.) She had also been watching a commercial for MD Anderson Cancer Hospital, which had something about melanoma. A few days later, she mentioned to my mother that I had that mole on the back of my leg. You can guess what happened next…. We (my mom and I) were in the doctor's office the next day getting it checked out.

*Can I just say that sometimes we don't want people in our lives messing with our lives!* I was a bit angry with my own daughter for mentioning that to my own mother. I figured it was nothing, and they were overreacting!

Guess what! They were *not* overreacting. I went to my family doctor, who the very same day sent me to the dermatologist. (I might add that this was close to five o'clock in the afternoon when most doctors are ready to leave.) The dermatologist squeezed me in before his quitting time.

Now let me tell you, my dermatologist is great. He has been a dermatologist for over thirty-five years. He wears a bow tie, and I'm only telling you this because I felt like, when he saw that mole on my leg, his little bow tie spun around about fifty times. You can imagine the shock and fear of the news he was going to have to tell this pregnant mama.

He took a biopsy that day, and the very next day, his nurse called me and said, "You have tested positive for melanoma cancer. We have scheduled you an appointment at MD Anderson Cancer Hospital in Houston, Texas. You will need to go next week. We are not equipped to handle pregnant patients with this!"

Whoa, whoa, whoa! This unassuming caterpillar was out in the open and had just been dive-bombed by the enemy! It was a crazy, unexpected, life-shaking moment in time, and it did not seem real.

How could this happen to me? I'm a good person! I go to church! I am a good wife and a good mom! For crying out loud, I teach special needs children for a living! What do I do now?

# 2

## GETTING TANGLED

The big, fat caterpillar starts to slow down and notice that something is not right in its body and mind. It feels like it is getting tangled as small threads start to trip it up, forming around its body.

It seems to me that sometimes either due to random events that happen to us out of the blue, or perhaps sometimes in our own faults, God allows us to go through sifting and trials. He knows exactly how to get your attention even if He has to totally knock the wind out of your sails and bring you to your knees, which is exactly where He needs you to be able to get your attention, to help you learn and grow and become not who you need to be, but who He called you to be. I quickly learned that sometimes what we see as a random happening is often the very thing that can put life on a path you never imagined, especially if you learn to put your trust in God!

Let me begin this chapter by giving a little prior knowledge. My husband and I grew up in church. We knew what "church" looked like, sounded like, and acted like, but can I say knowing "church" and knowing a loving Jesus are entirely two different things!

On that day, after I calmed down from my hormonal, pregnant, bad news breakdown, my husband and I prayed (I want to say, I am so thankful for my husband taking the time to pray with me and for me on that day. I am thankful he held my hands and told me it would be okay). We felt like God was saying to us, *"Here is your opportunity to walk the walk and not just talk the talk." In essence, we had a chance to press in to life with Jesus, to get to know what an amazing God He is, to let Him take us on an adventure of a lifetime. That is how we chose to look at our cancer journey from that day on!* Little did we know how our views on life would change. We were positive and upbeat, but I still had to tell my parents. My mother is an amazing woman, but I did have to tell her I did not want to hear anything negative or downcast. I knew that would be a challenge for her (she worries just as any mom would), but like I said, she is amazing, and she stuck to it. Both of my parents stuck to it and respected my wishes.

So began my metamorphosis process. I was once an unassuming caterpillar, but I needed God's threads of trust, provision, grace, joy, and love to wrap me up tight like a cocoon. I needed Him to do a great work in me, not just in my body, but in my heart, mind, and spirit.

I was getting tangled in expectation for whatever He had in store for me. Looking back, I realize how important that prayer was to set the tone for this life experience that would totally shake us and later shape us. The presence of mind my husband and I kept about how to approach this obstacle in life was a priceless treasure.

# 3

# THREADS OF TRUST

Imagine a limping, struggling caterpillar still trying to fight but realizing it might not make it on its own.

There we sat in the waiting room of the amazingly huge MD Anderson Cancer Hospital. After Houston driving, the maze of hallways, getting somewhat lost, and trying to read the itinerary of appointments and lab visits, we were sure the hard part was over (sense of humor is always very important). We waited a very long time and wanted to get impatient be we did maintain a good attitude.

I know God had His hand right in the middle of the situation. We were so blessed to have an amazingly knowledgeable and personable doctor. He was and still is a young gifted surgeon who has performed many cancer surgeries, yet he was surprised to see me at thirty-one years old and seven months pregnant as his patient. He took the utmost caution with me, took time to explain what the protocol would be for surgery and further testing. He also let me know we were going to forge a new path together, as he had never performed surgery on a pregnant patient. To be quite honest, he seemed happy to meet my husband and me as we were younger and seemed to have hopeful attitudes.

Later that day, I also met with an obstetrics doctor at a different hospital in Houston, which my doctor corresponded services with (MD did not have an OB-GYN doctor in their services). They performed an ultrasound and determined the baby was great and growing fine. The doctor then said she would be monitoring the baby during surgery and everything should be fine.

Wow, what a whirlwind of a day! Not only that, but I would have surgery the next day. (I want to make a special note to say in the midst of all of that, there was peace!) God was wrapping me in trust. I had to trust two doctors that I had just met to cut on me and monitor the other life in me! Most of all, I had to trust that God knew exactly what I needed.

The next day, surgery went very well. It was a wide excision biopsy that cut a deep and wide chunk out of my calf muscle and needed seventeen stitches. It was pulled very tight, and I spent a long four weeks of my pregnancy on crutches.

I would not be telling the truth if I said everything was just peachy. Real life sunk in real fast! For one thing: Your balance while pregnant is not the same, and to add crutches to that is a whole new level of difficulty. Second thing: I had a two-year-old at home that wanted to run and get into things, and I had a hard time getting to him. Third thing: I had to go back to work and teach. I had many children in my class who needed extra help keeping focus; I had to be on my feet a lot. Needless to say, God was giving me an overwhelming amount of things to trust Him for.

I find it quite remarkable that I could trust so many new people working on me, yet when I got back to my routine of doing things, I was having an extremely difficult time trusting that this was all working for my good.

I know my husband will never forget the day I was so frustrated with all of the things. I launched one of my crutches like a javelin across the backyard. We can laugh about it now, but it was all very real and raw on that day. Some things you just have to go through so you will develop good character and appreciate the good days. I have only had a few really bad days in my life, and that was one full of frustration that drove me straight to read my

Bible! By the way, on that day, I read:

> Not only so, but we also glory in our sufferings, because we know that suffering produces perseverance; perseverance, character; and character, hope. And hope does not put us to shame, because God's love has been poured out into our hearts through the Holy Spirit, who has been given to us.

**Romans 5:3-5**

I was kind of relieved that I read these words because I knew that God was building my character. On the other hand, I was kind of angry at the timing of all the building being done. All the more reason for me to trust!

After I got the stitches out, I was informed that no further testing would be done until six weeks after my baby was born. I now had a small window to get my mind right and get some sense of normalcy back in my home.

"Trust in the Lord with all your heart and lean not on your own understanding; in all your ways submit to him, and he will make your paths straight" (Proverbs 3:5-6).

# 4

# THREADS OF PROVISION

The caterpillar starts slowing down. It is anxious. It is somewhat scared. It knows change is coming, but it does not know how!

I have never been so thankful to see a school year end, and to be quite honest, I did not think I was going to have to go back after that year, so I gave up my position. I left on good terms, and I was so thankful for the teachers and staff that I worked with as they saw what I was going through and provided meals, groceries, and an amazing baby shower that provided diapers for my baby for over a year.

That summer was a beautiful time. We welcomed our son Max into the world. He was beautiful and healthy and had no signs of any cancer. I soon found out I would not be able to breastfeed him as I had done the rest of our children. This was due to the future testing I would have to do soon and the amounts of radioactive materials used to perform those tests. I was a bit apprehensive as his birth approached. I learned during my pregnancy that melanoma could possibly be passed from mother to baby through the placenta. To top it off, I had a nightmare of him being born with black spots all over him. I have no words to express how thankful to God we were that he was so healthy! He had big green eyes and a sweet demeanor. We noticed right away that he smiled at an earlier age than any of our other kiddos. I do not think that happened just by chance.

Once again, upon the birth of our baby, our church provided meal after meal for us, so much so that my children were so disappointed when I started cooking again. It was another way God shows He provides for people through people!

The summer progressed fine until the last week of July. After much agonizing, my husband told me we could not afford for me to stay home. I was so disappointed and a bit angry. I just wanted to be a mom and spend time with my children, who were thirteen, seven, two, and six weeks old. I felt like that was a job in itself and I was being cheated out of it! So I swallowed my pride, put aside my own agenda, and I went back to my previous school to see if they had any spots open for me to come back and teach.

It was too late in the summer, and the principal said they had filled all of the open positions, but like I said, I left on good terms, and she made a call to the principal of another elementary school that had a position open for kindergarten teacher. It was a position I was looking forward to, so I agreed to interview for it the next week.

In the meantime, that Tuesday of the same week, we left our older children with my parents. Quite honestly, I really do not think we could have made it through all this without my parents helping with our children. We live in the same town, and I know God had His hand right on them to be able to help us! My dad was going through some health challenges of his own, but my parents were and still are *always* willing to help when needed.

My husband, newborn son, and I drove to Houston, which is about an eight-hour drive from Norman, Oklahoma. Once again, provision was made for us. My mother's cousin happened to live in Houston, and when she found out we were coming for tests at MD, she most graciously opened her home and allowed us to stay not just then but every time we needed to come. I now realize because of her kindness, we saved thousands of dollars. God used her to show us true generosity, and I will never be able to thank her enough for her precious gift of hospitality.

I was scheduled to start further testing, which I

just knew was going to be fine, and I wouldn't have to go anymore…. The next day, I had all sorts of scans, and a dye tracer test was done to see if cancer was traveling to any other parts of my body.

It seemed to be traveling to my left hip, so the next day I had another biopsy done to remove about three lymph nodes from that hip to see if there were any cancer cells in them. It was just a same-day surgery, but it was a very long day for my husband and newborn in the lobby. It seems my baby cried for a very long time, and my husband was getting frustrated, as that was really the longest time he had ever spent with a newborn alone. I had always done the work on that end of the family. Needless to say, both were happy to see me when I came out of the recovery room.

I had about a three-inch incision on my hip that did not require any stitches, but it was still quite sore. I was told to take it easy and not be on my feet too much or lifting anything over a few pounds. You know where this is going….

Somebody had to take care of our baby while my husband was driving home that day. Somebody had to take kids here and there the next day. Somebody was trying to pretend like nothing was happening to her. Somebody was not asking for help. Somebody was doing too much in her own strength!

That Sunday, three days back from surgery, my mother-in-law had asked my children and me to go back-to-school shopping. She did not know all that was going on at the time, and I wasn't sure my husband wanted her to know, so I just pretended nothing was wrong. We met her at the mall, and I just ignored the pressure building in the hip incision. I pushed around the double stroller with my wiggly two-year-old and newborn. I quickly followed my thirteen-year-old daughter from store to store, trying not to argue about fashion differences, and tried to keep my seven-year-old son interested in clothes shopping when he just wanted to go to the toy store or the arcade. I also was trying to be gracious to my mother in law who was extending her kindness in paying for back-to-school clothes. Once again, provision was made for my children!

While going through the mall that day, I began to feel pressure in my hip. I toted my babies to the bathroom so I could check myself, and as I pulled down my jeans, lymph fluid squirted in about a six-inch stream out of my hip. I tried not to panic, but I quickly got a tissue to put over the incision. I then pushed my big stroller out of the bathroom and found my mother-in-law. I told her what was going on.

She was shocked and a bit angry that we had not shared the news of cancer with her. She offered to take us home. I just asked if she could bring the older kids home when they were done. I just did not want to alarm them. I took the babies with me and drove home.

I'm just stubborn, I guess. That can benefit me or hinder me, depending on the situation. In this situation, God allowed me to be strong and not panic. I got back to my home and rested as well as I could. I did not tell anybody, except my husband, about it until much later. After all, the next day, I had a job interview, and I had to look the part of a healthy teacher that could handle a class full of wormy kindergartners.

When I woke up, another stream of fluid squirted out of my hip. It was a little sore and feverish. I covered it with gauze, got dressed, and went to my interview. I had a good interview, and I got the job on the spot. School was starting in three weeks, and there was a lot to do. Yay…oh no!

When I left there, my skirt was completely wet with lymph fluid, so I quickly called my dermatologist's office, and they got me in ASAP, as they knew what was going on with my biopsy. He checked out my incision, and he told me there was an infection in it, probably from all of the running around I was doing when I was not supposed to.

On the same day, he sent me to the local surgeon, who quickly told me I was going to have to get to surgery to remove all of the infection that was spreading quickly.

I called my husband. He met me quickly and said, "Are you sure you have to have surgery again?" I know he was still traumatized by the waiting room with a crying newborn just a few days earlier. My husband called my parents, who were a bit upset at me for not taking it easy and letting them help more. Surgery went well. I had a bigger incision on top of my other one with stitches and a drain tube with a bulb to collect lymph fluid. I spent three days in the hospital.

At that time, I had to take it easy. I had to let people help, and I had to let people in to know what was going on. I had to let people pray for me. I had numerous aunts, uncles, friends, and family members come visit me and pray for me.

That does not sound that hard, but it was! I had kids to

take care of and play with, a husband that needed a strong, beautiful wife, and a brand new job to prepare for! I did not have time for this mess.

I got home from the hospital on a Saturday. My mother stayed at my house just to make sure I did not overdo it with the kids. I was so thankful for her, as I was feeling pretty bad. That lasted a day or two, but I really had to get better quick, as I would need to report to school on Wednesday for teacher workdays and meetings.

In retrospect, I can see God meeting every need, tangling me in His threads of provision:

- Threads of provision for my health through knowledgeable doctors that corresponded back and forth from Norman and Houston.

- Threads of provision for my spirit through friends and family holding me in prayer.

- Threads of provision of wisdom in my husband having employment with our insurance company and knowing what to do and how it all works.

- Threads of provision of normalcy for my children surrounded by loving grandparents and family members.

He supplied all of our needs. He was just not doing it how we planned. I quickly learned God's ways are not my ways.

"Surely God is my help: the Lord is the one who sustains me" (Psalm 54:4).

# 5

# A SQUIRMING WORM

A lonely caterpillar beginning the process of a cocoon with small web-like threads hanging out of its body, just dangling upside-down under a leaf, blowing in the breeze, and subject to predators.

A squirming, writhing, desperate worm—that is exactly what I felt when I got the call from MD Anderson on Monday! It was my surgeon's nurse. It was *not* good news! My biopsy came back with cancer cells in all lymph nodes taken from my hip. I would have to go back to Houston in about three weeks for another much bigger surgery to remove most of the lymph nodes in my left hip.

The predator was my mind! I had just had two surgeries in the previous week! I just got the drain out of my leg the day before! I have to get kids ready for school. I have babies to prepare to go to child care. I have a classroom to prepare at a new school. I did not have time for this in my life! Fear was running rampant in my mind.

All I knew to do was call my husband to pray. My husband is the voice of reason most of the time, but on this day, he just made me mad! I guess I was just looking for sympathy and for him to hold me in my "woe is me" moment. He did not provide it. He told me to quit feeling sorry for myself; I was going to be fine, God had me covered, and we were going to keep good attitudes about it. It was just something we would get through. He was just so nonchalant about it, and my mind was freaking out.

Those are all good things…but this is exactly where my mind went, *Oh yeah, well, you are not the one who has just had two surgeries in a week, and you are not the one getting cut on again in a few weeks, and you are not the one who gets up with babies in the middle of the night, and you are not the one who is going to go into a class of kindergartners who need a teacher who is fun and energetic, and….* You get the picture!

I am just going to say grace was on me that day (it may not seem like it), but I did not say a single one of those things out loud to my husband; I stuffed it. I needed comfort, but he was not going to provide it, and quite honestly, I wanted to run and tell on him for being completely insensitive. I knew enough not to tell anyone, as I did not want them to think badly of my husband; after all, only I could do that. Hahaha.

# <u>6</u>

# THREADS OF COMFORT

The caterpillar is firmly planted but dangling upside down on a branch with silken threads starting to cover most of its body like a snuggly, comfy blanket.

Can I just say this is a setup! In this moment and circumstance in which nobody could console or know exactly how to make me feel better, God knew exactly what I was going to do. *I ran to Him! I sat in His lap! I told on my husband! I threw a fit! I cried! I prayed! I read His word!*

I had finally come to the end of myself and reached to my Heavenly Father. I was no longer going to be able to ride the coattails of my husband's faith. I was going to have to do this myself. I was going to have to have a more personal relationship with Jesus. I was going to have to talk to Him every day and let Him speak to me through His Word.

When I realized this, I felt like a little girl safe in the comfort of her daddy's lap. He put my face right in His hands and softly spoke through His words in the Bible. I'm not ashamed to say I was reading a children's Bible. It was easy to understand, and I took Him at His word. That day He told me I was fearfully and wonderfully made (Psalm 139:14). I was more than a conqueror (Romans 8:37). If I would draw close to Him, He would always draw close to me (James 4:8). His power is made perfect in my weakness (2 Corinthians 12:9). I believed Him, and I still do.

I do believe the most important word I found and dwelt on that day was one that said, "For God has not given us a spirit of fear, but of power and of love and of a sound mind" (2 Timothy 1:7, NKJV). I rolled that around in my mind because my mind was not sound. It was quite the opposite. I then thought about the words I had heard in church about the devil roaming about like a roaring lion, seeking someone to devour (1 Peter 5:8). Suddenly I realized that the fear was the enemy that was relentlessly overtaking me, roaring at me, pawing at me, and it was not from God. I knew I had a very real enemy after my life and I had better, under no certain terms, command him to get away! I had better start boldly declaring my power, love, and sound mind! I had better recognize I had God as my strength and my shield, and my heart would trust Him (Psalm 28:7).

Now the matter of my husband, he was right! Yes, I said it! He was right! The Bible told me everything he had just tried to tell me, perhaps a little sweeter, but still the same thing. I forgave him even though he never knew he hurt my feelings or I was mad. However, I learned to just go straight to God's words in matters when I need comfort and encouragement. I decided I would not feel sorry for myself. I would have a bright, positive attitude! I would show love. I would be powerful. I would have a sound mind! I knew I could do it with God's help. I was going to have to do my part to believe it!

"And I will ask the Father, and he will give you another advocate to help you and be with you forever" (John 14:16).

# 7

# THREADS OF GRACE

The caterpillar is mostly wrapped up in the soft threads of its cocoon. It is only able to be still and listen to God whisper.

When I had finally brought myself around, I spoke to my husband and told him my feelings about how I felt like maybe it was just not the right timing for this new job. It was not fair to little students in their first year of school to have their teacher gone so much in the beginning. He agreed. We did not know all the details, but we knew things would work out.

The next day I went to my new school to tell my new principal what was happening. I told her I did not feel like it would be beneficial or fair to a class full of kindergarteners for their teacher to have to be gone for the first weeks of school when it is so important for them to learn class and school procedures. Quite honestly, I was not sure how long I would have to be gone, and I did not want to start the year like that.

She was shocked, and she could tell I was on the verge of tears. She thought about it for a moment, hugged me, and thanked me for being thoughtful and truthful. She then asked me if I would consider a part-time position as their gifted resource coordinator. This was not a classroom position, and it would not be so stressful and stringent in planning if I had to be gone.   I would have to learn a lot for the position, but I took it because my family needed the income.   No doubt God's ease and grace to that situation were at play. I started a new school year with a new, new position and a heavyweight of an upcoming major surgery looming in the distance.

Not only did grace find me in my job but with my children. My parents once again saw the need in my budget and offered to watch the two little boys while I taught. I never wanted them to have to do that! At the time, it was the best option, and I was so thankful for relieving my mind of mommy guilt because I knew my boys were getting the best care possible!

The next weeks were *busy*! My mind was torn in a thousand directions. It was probably a very good thing I was preparing for a new job, as it kept my mind on something different than the current situation. Life goes on, even in chaos, even in sadness. Possibly the very best thing I could do was just shift focus.

I began the first few weeks of the new school year feeling like my own children were off to a great start and also getting to know new students. It was difficult figuring out what my schedule for the year would look like. I enjoyed the fact that it was part-time as sometimes I went in a few hours in the morning or sometimes a few hours in the afternoon. Oftentimes, it gave me a break from thinking about my situation, and quite honestly, it was easier on my mom guilt, as I was more available for my children.

Soon came the first week of September. I had to report back to MD Anderson for another much bigger surgery! This time it would be my dad and mom, my toddler and infant, and me making the journey to Houston. My husband stayed at home as he needed to work and be with the two older children who did not need to miss a full week of school to sit at a hospital. The trip was a good one with lots of stops for my little boys. I must say I was a bit nervous about this surgery, and I guess that is to be expected. I was not the one who was supposed to be needing all of the extra help; I was usually the one helping, teaching, loving kids, and it was going to be somewhat hard to take it easy. I had to go directly to the hospital for a quick check-in with my doctor and some bloodwork. Pre-op instructions were given, and I knew this was going to be a big deal; however, I tend to be obnoxiously optimistic and sometimes borderline superwoman, so I thought I would be able to handle what was coming with no problems whatsoever! I hoped!

I was so thankful for my family with me at this time, as my mind did need to decompress and prepare for what was to come. Once again, we were so blown away by my most gracious cousin, who opened her home to us and cooked delicious meals for us, and just became the biggest blessing we could have ever asked for in this whole adventure. You know the saying, "God blesses people through people." That could not be more true! I could not think of a better example of hospitality in this time when I just needed to not worry so much about the little things.

Surgery day. We arrived early and got checked in. I kissed and played with my babies until they called me back. I even got to spend time with my sister, who had come up from her home in Rockport, Texas. I thought it was so nice of her to be there. She was an amazing help with my little ones while they were in the waiting room.

After they took me back for surgery, I do not remember much except waking up in the recovery room with chills and an excruciating pain in my left hip and thigh. Of course, I was all packed in and sewn up tightly with two long drain tubes coming out of my leg.

I remember the nurses trying to move me over to the recovery bed and telling me to push on that left leg to scoot over.

Let me tell you…I have a very high pain tolerance. I was once a high-level gymnast who had overcome injuries. I had given birth four times, and I know what pain feels like, but I had *never* and hope to *never* again feel physical pain like *that*! I cried loudly as I moved, and I finally made it to that bed. I just laid there and wept. I was not really sure I would ever be the same person of physical prowess I was before.

The surgery was to remove most of the lymph nodes from my left hip. However, in order to do that, they had to cut deep and across the main tendons in the front of that hip. The ones that help you lift your leg up and down and side to side, and I am sure they had to dig out most of those nodes. I had a ten-inch incision from the top of my hip to the middle of my thigh. It was going to be a long recovery.

I just remember thinking, *Jesus, help, Jesus, help, Jesus, help!* That is really all I could pray in recovery. I remember my sister and my brother coming in to see me, and I'm sure they were worried, but they always have managed to make me feel better and get a smile out of me. Really they just told me how my little ones were doing in the waiting room and kept the conversation light, and I really could not concentrate very well to talk for too long.

I was in the hospital for three days after that! It was a long three days, but I really needed it as I would have to get used to walking with all the tubes hanging out of my leg. I was also going to have to figure out how to hold babies and do daily work with these things for the next few weeks.

There are specifically three things I remember about my hospital stay. The first one is that MD Anderson is, in my opinion, the definition of world peace. It is doctors and nurses of all races and backgrounds working with people all over the world with one common purpose, which is to eradicate the evil of cancer. I know that is a heavy thought, but as I saw people, some sadly old pros at cancer treatment, and some on the new journey (men, women, children of all colors), I felt like I was in the right place for treatment and healing.

The second and third lessons are much lighter thoughts. Like learning that getting a shot in your belly is way better than any other place you can get one. I didn't know how very helpful this little gem of pain management would be until I began my therapy treatment and had to give myself shots. I learned this thanks to a very kind and patient nurse, who talked me through the process and convinced me to try it.

The third thing is that the more you get up and move, the better and quicker you will heal. I kind of already knew this as a former athlete who was no stranger to sore muscles. It totally made sense to me that I had to move, but I had never had an incision like this one. I will say that the first time I had to get up and try to walk and put pressure on that left leg, I puked about three times! It really made me sick to my stomach. Thank God for fearless nurses who were kind enough, and patient enough, and encouraging (stubborn) enough to just let me throw up and get right back up and try it again. That was just the first day, but by the third day, I could get around pretty well, and I walked around every chance I got because I was ready to get back home.

My parents and babies came to see me every day.

I could not wait to see them and hold them and let my two-year-old press the buttons on my bed and for the TV channels. I have to say I was a little depressed because I was not sure how I was going to be able to do everything that needed to be done. I am a very hands-on parent, and I really like to be on the move with my kids at the park, on the trampoline, walking around the neighborhood. I would much rather be up and doing something useful than sitting in front of the TV for a long time.

On my release from the hospital, I still had the drains coming out of my leg, which I would have for the next two weeks. I could walk slowly, and I got tired easily, which also meant I got frustrated with myself easily because I was having to rely on my parents heavily for the care of my babies, and it was just *hard* because I had so much guilt and anger at myself. It was a much longer ride home, it seemed, than the one going.

I specifically remember a stop we made at Dairy Queen in Huntsville, Texas, on our way back home. Granted, this was not very far from Houston, but with two babies, we just needed to get out and move a little bit. I was still in my gown and robe with drain tubes coming out of my leg and hooked in the pocket of my robe, and of course, pale and moving slow. I sat down at the table, and the people sitting across from us really must have been troubled by my appearance and all that was going on with my parents trying to help take care of my babies. They waited a while, and then they came over and asked about the situation and if they could pray over me. I immediately said yes, and right there in Dairy Queen, they prayed for me. I was a bit embarrassed but totally blown away by their boldness to see a need and pray for it right then and there. I thought about how many times I have said to people, "I'm praying for you," and not actually taken the time to hold their hands or place a hand on them and let them actually hear words of prayer and encouragement. Now I know that I will never see those people again, but the fact that they did that for me has changed the way I think about prayer and the urgency of being bold and just doing it right then so people can feel the comfort and power of a loving, life-giving God. I am so glad God allowed me to experience that lesson firsthand when I needed it most in my life!

Upon arriving home, I was greeted by my husband and other two children, who I'm sure were quite taken back by the amount of staples and tubes still coming out of my body. They were happy to see me and were very helpful for the weeks to come.

I did stay at my home during the night the first week, and my mom and dad would come and get the little boys and me and take us to their house during the day to help me out. It was a crash course in letting people help my stubborn self and me. I did shed a few tears thinking the healing process was not moving fast enough.

I must say my own parents gave me some great practical advice and I still use it today. It was, "Just do what you can do, and don't worry about the rest. It will take care of itself." Also, "Let people help you because if you do not let people help, you deny them of a blessing!"

I was soon reminded of God's grace that says, "Come to Me, rest in Me. I have already done the work you are worried about. It will be better than you could ever

imagine!" I would like to say this was easy for me, but it
*was not*. I had to really fight the inner voices that said, "You
are worthless to your family right now!" "Your husband is
going to look for someone else to love him!" "Your babies
are not going to want to be around you anymore." I have to
say I was a bit short-sighted because, in the grand scheme
of life, a six week recovery time is not that long, but when I
was constantly having to battle my mind and my body was
hurting, it was hard to see how all of this was going to play
out and to remember to be farsighted in the vision for my
life.

I had to discipline myself to not listen to that
negativity. Just as I had told my own parents, I did not want
to hear anything negative; this was my own mind running
rampant, and it was relentless. I had to constantly rely on
what I knew of God's character. I had to quickly learn to
lean into His grace even though I was not sure how to or
even what it really was to accept the things I could not get
done in my own strength, to let people help. It was more
difficult than I could imagine, but through the process, I
gained compassion for people who struggle with health
issues, and I gained an enormous respect for caregivers
who patiently attend appointments, listen to doctors, and
put their lives on hold to take care of loved ones.

Without God's grace, my life would be a shambles,
and honestly, I would probably be dead. I was very hard
on myself, borderline drill sergeant trying to push myself
to constantly do better. I was fearful and prideful to think
things wouldn't get done unless I did them myself. It was
a very hard time for me to let go. I felt worthless. I really
had to shift my focus to Jesus, dig in his words, and seek

his wisdom in this specific time and situation. I read these beautiful words and clung to them:

> Praise the Lord, my soul and forget not all his benefits□who forgives all your sins and heals all your diseases, who redeems your life from the pit and crowns you with love and compassion, who satisfies your desires with good things so that your youth is renewed like eagle's. The Lord works righteousness and justice for all the oppressed.

**Psalm 103:1-6**

These words were so eye-opening for me and very timely in their delivery. I think I began to learn truly what grace is. As I looked and meditated on those verses of scripture, it gave me a much clearer picture. I saw a God who loves me so deeply that He is willing to be all of these things (forgiver, healer, redeemer, crowner, satisfier, worker of righteousness and justice) for me. All of these things I cannot be for myself no matter how hard I try! I just need to see Him as all of those things, and my jobs are to praise Him and be renewed. It was and still is so refreshing to know that my amazing God wants me to enjoy the life I have been given through His grace, which is a much better way to live.

# 8

# THREADS OF PERSPECTIVE

The caterpillar is fully covered by a blanket of tight threads. It cannot move; all it can do is talk to God and listen to God speak! *This is possibly the most important time in a caterpillar's life.*

I would love to say that every day I stayed in that grace, and I remembered that verse, and there was no way the grinds of life could ever get me down as long as I remembered His words. I know that is not realistic, especially when the enemy seems to be attacking from all sides. I was really trying very hard to battle to feel better physically and mentally. I studied God's words. I wanted to use them in my life just like the armor of a mighty warrior. I was getting more proficient in remembering verses. This helped me tremendously as my tormenting inner thoughts would come. I was starting to defend against them with the truth of the scriptures I was equipping myself with. I was growing spiritual muscles and learning to put up my shield when the fiery darts would come. Perhaps one of the most eye-opening prayers I prayed was for His perspective.

I specifically remember trying to take a shower in my second week after surgery. I was just standing there looking at myself. I still had a hip full of staples and two drain tubes coming out of my leg. I was getting around pretty well, but there was still a lot of pain. As I started the shower, I had a quiet moment to talk with God; I just said, "God, please, if You can, help me find the good in this because right now I feel like this really sucks!" About that time, my two-year-old had come into the bathroom with me and began poking at the shower curtain and trying to climb in with me. I also had my little three-month-old sleeping in his carrier in the bathroom with me, and he had woken up and started crying. I said, "God, I need Your perspective on this. I am having trouble!"

I felt, as clear as day, He said, "This is not just for you. This is for the people around you. This is for your daughter to see a woman that can be tough in Me, who can show her how to believe the best in all situations and can go through tough times with faith, grace, and perseverance! This is for these little boys fussing at your side. They will not remember this time, but from now on, they will have a mom who will praise Me and celebrate life and find good things in each day! They will be strong because you will teach them to love Me! This is for your parents, who sometimes waver in faith, to know I'm real and I'm working! This is for your husband to develop compassion, partnership, and wisdom in how to lead this family! This is for those who know you and who will know you in the future, who will hear My story through your experience and will be drawn to know more of My love and compassion and kindness!"

God was so faithful to share His perspective with me, and from that time, I have not forgotten that most of the things that God allows us to go through are not just for us, but for those around us, watching us to see where our strength is coming from, to hear about how God pulled us through, and to be an encouragement to those who may go through a similar situation.

I gained God's perspective that day, and I know my tears and my pain are never wasted. I have never looked at trials the same way.

> Consider it pure joy, my brothers and sisters, whenever you face trials of many kinds, because you know that the testing of your faith produces perseverance. Let Perseverance finish its work so that you may be mature and complete, not lacking anything. If any of you lacks wisdom, you should

ask God, who gives generously to all without finding fault, and it will be given to you.

**James 1:2-5**

"For our present troubles are small and won't last very long, yet they produce for us a glory that vastly outweighs them and will last forever" (2 Corinthians 4:17, NLT).

# 9

# THREADS OF PRAYER AND PERSEVERANCE

Picture a caterpillar in a cocoon for the duration of metamorphosis. Things are being stripped away. Things are being added to it. Things are changing, and it is a long process of hanging in there and waiting!

Week three after this major surgery, I was feeling better. I did not have any sick days left, and it was only September, so I felt like I needed to try to go back to work. I still had staples and drains in my hip and thigh, but I just figured if I went slow and worked a few hours, I would be alright.

Looking back at this time, I really should not have done it, but sometimes you feel like you have to do what you have to do for your family. I wore a long skirt and pinned my drain tubing up on the inside of it. I wore a long shirt and sensible shoes and went to work. I made it through the day, although no one told me I was going to have recess duty which was a long walk from my classroom and a bit dangerous as you never know when a small child might bump into you or come running for a low hug around your waist. I have to say I was probably pretty worthless at my duty that day, but I did manage to blow my whistle and get each class lined up to go back inside. I was worn out from the stress of it, and I was quite happy to be leaving by 12:45 that day. I made it through a week of work like that, but I was able to find someone to cover my duty for the rest of that week.

The following week I went back to Houston for a day to get the staples and tubes out of my leg. At that point, a diagnosis of *stage four metastatic melanoma cancer* was given. That sounds very menacing, but can I just say there are times when God shields our brains? He does it for our own protection, and there has never been a saying more true for me in this time than "ignorance is bliss." Being thirty-one years old and not knowing much at all about cancer, I did not know what that meant, and honestly, I was too busy in my life with my family and job to even want to look it up or ask about it. It did not scare me because, again, I did not know about it. I just knew I had a healing God who is always with me, and it was just something I was making it through.

It was not until a few years down the road that I became aware that most of the time, stage four is oftentimes the final stage of terminal cancer.

In week six after my surgery, I began my chemo treatment, which was interferon A, an immunotherapy drug. It would consist of the first six weeks of having to go to my oncologist's office to be hooked up to an IV of the drug for about an hour each day. I will say I was definitely one of the younger patients in there, and when I told the nurses I had a now four-month-old baby and three other children, they looked on me with much pity. They did not sugarcoat how this treatment would make me feel. They also made sure I had a good support of family and friends to help me if I was feeling low. After the first six weeks of IVs, I would have to give myself shots of interferon three times a week for a solid year. I would have to check in with the oncologist's office every two weeks. I went to Houston every three months for scans.

The title for this book was birthed in an MRI tunnel which I fondly refer to as my cocoon, where I talked to God and always felt like He was right with me, bringing comfort, joy, and strength in a perilous situation. I knew His hands were working most when I was still. He knows every centimeter of my body, and I trusted Him to be my God and do the work He needed to do in me.

In the first few weeks of treatment, I would have flu-like symptoms of fever, chills, and headaches. It was just in the evening, a few hours after treatment. I felt like I was doing pretty well with it. I was able to work and take care of my family. I had only a few times when I just could not get it together. I must say I had tons of family and friends praying for me. I know on several days, I was not making it on my own strength but on the prayers for strength everyone was praying for me.

By the sixth month of treatment, it was beginning to wear on my body. Just little things felt like really big things. I also was not resting very well, as my baby was not yet a good sleeper. My body ached all of the time, and I had mouth sores continuously for about three months. I lost quite a lot of weight, and I was just tired. By April in the school year, my part-time job of teaching felt like it was full-time, and I was struggling just to make it those few hours I was there.

I really was trying my best to be positive for my children and my husband, but some days I felt like I had been hit by a Mack Truck, and it was all I could do to just get out of bed. I would love to say that all of the scriptures and warm fuzzy feelings of loving God were with me all of the time, but they were not, and my faith was so fickle. It just seemed like a wobbly game of Jenga. Some days I felt so strong, like I could handle everything coming at me, and then some days low, down and out, and totally a sobbing mess.

During this time, there was such a heaviness in my spirit, and I will say the battle in my mind was *raging*! Many days I contemplated just giving up. My reasoning was that my treatment was costing my family so much money, I was not able to give my attention fully to my family, and I was not able to keep up with my home like I thought I should be able to do. I was not the teacher I thought I should be, and I was not living the strong, victorious life I thought I should be living. I was not exemplary. I just mean my life was not a shining example of what I thought a Christian life should look like.

Then one day, I heard a sermon that said something along the lines of, "We are all broken people, and our work and our lives will not be perfect until we get to heaven, but the brokenness of life is so valuable to Jesus and allows us to be relatable to others who struggle. Life is what it is! It is often dirty and sad, and if people judge or can't have compassion, then it is their problem, and they need Jesus too." I just remember thinking, *All of this time, I have been trying to be so perfect. Trying to make my life something worth looking at, but right now, it is broken, ugly, and weak!* The message was very freeing to me. I allowed our church prayer partners to pray over me every time I felt that heaviness come on me.

I realized I needed to really press in and remember the very real fact that I could do all of the things I was doing was a miracle. I continued to serve in church in the nursery. Two of my children were there, and I felt a sense of duty to serve in that area. I also began to serve as a prayer partner in hopes people could feel God's love, comfort, and power through me, just as I had every time I needed prayer. During this time, I had prayer partners at church and also family and friends lifting me in prayers. I am fully aware *that my strength was indeed supernatural!*

In an effort to find things to be thankful and excited for, I felt like it was necessary to begin making lists. I made one for all of the things I would like to do, the places I would like to travel to, the people I would like to meet. I found that writing was a great mind relief for me when I had time to do it. I love poetry and children's literature. I even found a funny little children's story I had written for my seven-year-old son when he was younger and long before this time in my life. Something I had always wanted to do that was near and dear on my bucket list of sorts was to have a children's book published.

I set about researching publishing companies to send it to as I had heard the process of having a book published can be brutal. So I just had a little faith and sent it to a company. I just felt like I needed to go for it. At least I tried, and I did not have much to lose if they did not like it. It turns out they did like the story and even asked if I had illustrations to go with it. Now I do not in any way claim to be an artist or an illustrator, but I whipped out some pictures for them in about three days for the book. They were not great illustrations, but enough to get the point across of what I was writing about. My friends and family were so excited about it, and we celebrated! I know it was a small victory, but it provided an overwhelming amount of joy and hope for the future.

I do not remember much about that year of teaching other than it was just hard to focus, and the people were very kind to me. I just plowed through and did what I needed to do to bring home a paycheck that was not really very big but helped a lot. I know that sounds horrible for a teacher to say, but my heart was not in it, and quite honestly, I did not feel physically capable to keep up the pace. I was really hoping to be able to stay home with my little ones for the next year.

# 10

# THREADS OF JOY AND STRENGTH

The caterpillar is still in the cocoon. It is tired from turmoil, but it is gaining strength. It is starting to look and think differently about its life and purpose. Not much longer will it stay in this cocoon. It needs to hear a few precious words from the Creator.

I was so hopeful that I would be able to stay home with my family for the next school year. I prayed for it every day in that time. I just did not think I could keep up the pace of being mom and teacher and wife. I did not feel like I was doing a very good job at any of them. That is when the bomb dropped on me. I am quite sure it was not a pleasant conversation my husband wanted to have with me, but in short, medical bills were adding up, we had four amazing children that needed things, and I was going to have to go to work full time for the next year!

I did not say much; I just remember being internally angry with my husband and just not talking to him. A few days after that conversation, I was up in the middle of the night with my baby, who was now about nine months old. He had also woken up my other son, who by this time was three years old. We sat on the couch, and I was just patting both of them, trying to get them back to sleep. I was so tired and even angrier. *I shook my fist at God! I said, "You see this, I am worn out! I am tired! There is no way I can go and teach full-time! You are going to have to do something about this right now!"*

Some people may say that I should not yell at God, but who else was going to help me? Quite honestly, I think He needs to know we are relying on Him and not ourselves for help. I needed Him to work in my life at that very moment, and I needed Him to know I was serious.

Okay, this next part is going to sound a little crazy. I will say when God talks to me, it will be in words I relate to and understand. It will be very practical for encouragement, just a word that prompts a thought or scripture.

So what I heard was "*Popeye*. Where does your strength come from?"

You see, *Popeye* was my favorite cartoon growing up. He was strong on his own and always wanted to do good, but he also knew what to do when he got weak and in trouble. Now I'm not suggesting that God was telling me to call out for spinach, *but He needed me to call on what I knew of His words!*

I quickly said, "The joy of the Lord is my strength!" When I said that out loud, it was spiritual spinach for my soul. I felt a rush, and every scripture I knew about joy and strength and praise and protection came flooding into my mind. I sang, and I praised Him because I remembered to put on a garment of praise for the spirit of heaviness. For the first time in almost a year, I did not feel tired. As a matter of fact, I stayed up most of the night and the next day just looking at scriptures and meditating on them and getting them deep in my soul so that I could battle the spirit of heaviness and any fiery darts it threw my way.

I determined that day to be joyful for the rest of my life. Would you believe the very next week, I was sitting in the waiting room at my oncologist's office, and I got a call from the principal of the school where I worked previously? She offered me a full-time teaching position as a second-grade teacher for the next year. I took it on the spot. I did not have to waste time applying for jobs, my God supplied my needs, and He showed me that He was giving me strength to do the job.

I ended my current part-time position in a much better and happier spot than when I started. I left that school on good terms. I was extremely happy for the summer break so that I could be with my family. As I continued my chemo shots, it was much less stressful knowing I was not going to have to rush around and plow through the day. We just spent the summer with a lot of trips to the park and some family reunions. My children's book also came out with the first copy that August, and we celebrated life and found something joyful in every day!

So we began a new school year with a supercharge. I had nineteen very eager and challenging second graders and four eager children of my own, now ages one, three, eight, fourteen. We were making it work and thriving! Each day had its challenges, but for the most part, all were growing and learning, and their teacher and mom was finding new strength and joy working full time.

My class was selected to welcome Japanese Dignitaries from the Hitachi Corporation. We had been learning about Oklahoma as it was the centennial celebration of our state. We taught them a few things about that and sang some songs for them, and they were quite impressed. My class required a tremendous amount of energy, as many of the students in my class were also special needs children. Like I said, I was bound and determined to be joyful and optimistic, and I believe those children could and would learn the things they needed to know for third grade and be successful!

By November of the year, I had finished my interferon shots, and I did not have to go back to Houston until April for scans. I felt like I was in the clear, and all was going well. When I went for scans in April, all was not well. I remember sitting with my reading group at school when I got the call. I had another teacher in my room helping, so I asked her if I could go ahead and take the call.

My surgeon said, "We need you to come to have more surgery to remove the main inguinal node and about three other nodes around it from that left hip, up higher in your abdomen area." There were still traces of cancer, but he felt confident that would take care of it. They needed me to get that done the first week of May, which was the very next week. Of course, my mind and reason said, *Can we wait until the end of May when school is out?* But the reason of my doctor said, "Let's get this taken care of right now." I tried very hard to hold it together in the hallway. I could feel my face getting hot, and I just lost it. I was so tired of bad news and just ready to move on and live my life.

I made my way to the school office to tell my principal and office managers I would not be able to complete the school year. I quite possibly have never felt as much sympathy and warmth from my school family as they reassured me everything in my classroom would be fine, and there was already a seasoned retired teacher ready to help take over my classroom until the summer.

I had about a week to prepare my lesson plans for my class and prepare my family for my absence. I'm glad it was a busy time and kept my mind off my situation and shifted focus to others. That in itself is another very important lesson for when you are feeling low or worried.

This time I left all of my children with my parents. I would just be gone about four days, so my husband took me this time. Surgery went well. It left me with another beautiful four-inch scar across the top of my hip, but I was able to move much easier than the big surgery, and my recovery was much quicker. The main thing I had to be excited about was that no more chemo would be needed, and all was well for now. I would go back for scans in October.

The summertime was one to remember. We celebrated our daughter's fifteenth birthday in the middle of June with a huge party. One we will never forget, as my mother-in-law had spent the last three years planning for the quinceañera. I'm only telling this because it is a very formal and traditional ceremony that has so many beautiful pieces to learn. I believe it was a miracle of healing in my body that just four weeks after surgery, I began teaching fifteen boys and fifteen girls a formal dance they would have to do for the ceremony. The fact that most of them were thirteen to sixteen years old and paid enough attention to learn it was miraculous in itself! It was a very fun time of formality, ceremony, and a huge party celebration.

"A cheerful heart is good medicine, but a crushed spirit dries up the bones" (Proverbs 17:22). Another way to think of this is, if you are cheerful, you feel good, but if you are sad, you hurt all over. My studies of joy and strength continued and still continue today. It seems you cannot have one without the other. I can attest to this first hand. The more I chose to be joyful and celebrate often, the better I felt in my body and spirit. I just felt like I was getting stronger in my faith, my mind, and my body.

I had so much to be joyful about at this time. The very next week, we moved into our "dream house," where we still live today. I'm using the term "dream house" cautiously, as it was and still is a fixer-upper. However, it is the most comfortable and, most importantly, functional house for a family like mine with several children and much activity!

By the end of the summer, I was offered a new position at my same school as a special education teacher (just like when I first began teaching there). I was excited and ready once more to begin another year after such a joyful and blessed summer.

Joy is a choice! The day is what you make it! If I learned anything, this might be the most valuable lesson. Circumstances are uncertain, health is uncertain, but I can always find a reason to be joyful. Because I am joyful, I praise God. Even if all is not going well, I praise God. I desire to be in the presence of God every day. I choose to be joyful every day. When I feel sad or low, I crank up the worship music either on the radio or singing. I sing at the top of my lungs, and sometimes I dance for God. Every time I do this, I physically feel better! I know my strength is constantly being renewed because of it. "Splendor and majesty are before him; strength and joy are in his dwelling place" (1 Chronicles 16:27).

I returned to Houston in November for another round of scans, this time CT and MRI scans looking at my total body. The MRI of my brain revealed three small spots that the doctor was concerned about. My husband and I just looked at each other like it was just a new part of the adventure, but we really did not think too much about it until we heard the process of how they wanted to treat those spots with radiation in which a metal halo would be screwed into my skull, and radiation waves would be guided to those spots. I was to have this done the very next day.

My faith was growing, and I was no longer wavering and getting tossed about. Lessons had been learned, perhaps the hard way and with a learning curve, but after you take the test a few times, you learn the material. I feel like this news would have really shaken us up a bit earlier in the process, but for some reason, just knowing what God's word says about worry and fear, I was not going to waste another second of my life doing that.

My husband and I prayed a peaceful and calm prayer together, and my attitude was this: *If I have to go through it, I will! If I live, I win! If I die, I win! I know Jesus! I will be joyful no matter what comes!*

The next morning, we began the process of checking in and talking to doctors who had performed this process many, many times. They walked us through the process of what was going to happen, and when it came time to attach the halo to my skull, my husband had to go back to the waiting room.

I was reasonably concerned as the nurse was rubbing the cotton swab across my forehead and getting ready to shave some spots where they would attach the screws on the back of my head. I had one song running through my brain at the time. It was "You Never Let Go" by artist Matt Redman. This seemed to be my anthem song as I was going through all of this. I would often catch myself singing it during MRIs and CT scans because I always felt like God was right with me in there. There He was right with me again in the valley of the shadow of death, and His perfect love was casting out my fear.

Just about that time, two other doctors entered the room and said, "We have been looking at your scans, and it looks like the spots are getting smaller, and one is gone altogether, so at this time, there is no need to go through this radiation process! *You are free to go!*"

# 11

# BURST FORTH

"I will not die but live, and will
proclaim what the LORD has done."

**Psalm 118:17**

The caterpillar has been squeezed, stripped-down,
scarred, and positively transformed as it burst out of its
cocoon—a new beautiful creation with wet wings and a
most optimistic disposition.

*You are free to go!* The words just kept echoing, just like someone screaming across a canyon! They did not have to tell me twice. I gathered my things quickly and headed out to the waiting room, where my husband looked at me with puzzled eyes. I told him what had just transpired in that room and we found ourselves in *awe* of the miracle just done right before our very eyes!

We left that waiting room so fast I'm sure heads were spinning. *I was just unable to contain my joy, so I turned cartwheels down the hall of MD Anderson Cancer Hospital.*

I am not sure my words are even in any way sufficient enough to explain the relief, joy, excitement, possibly even disbelief at my life at that moment. It is one of the things you hope for, but when it happens, you just think nobody is going to believe this! The good news is I believed it, and my husband believed it, and we hung on to and still hang on to the healing power of our God!

At that moment, the bonds of sickness, weakness, and poverty of thoughts were broken off of me.

"But he said to me, 'My grace is sufficient for you, for my power is made perfect in weakness.' Therefore I will boast all the more gladly about my weakness, so that Christ's power may rest on me" (2 Corinthians 12:9).

Through no power of my own, but to Christ be the glory for healing in my body and mind!

Would you believe what was supposed to be a week-long trip to Houston turned out to be a day trip as we happily flew standby on the way back home?

Life-changing…I will never be the same because

of this experience God used to show my weakness and His power and glory.

I am quite sure I did not share this part of my story freely enough with people. I shared it with my church family and with my own family, but perhaps by writing this book and sharing my story, many more people can come to know the awesome power and goodness of a loving Heavenly Father.

My journey began as an unassuming, little, insignificant caterpillar. I was just a woman, just a wife, just a mom, just a teacher. I did not believe I was important enough for God to reach out to me. Yet perhaps sometimes I thought I was too important, so much so that I could do everything myself. Basically, I was just doing my job as a human being, just crawling along, sometimes trudging through my duties and responsibilities. Little did I know that through my weakness, God could make my life so much better than I could even ask or think!

Then one day, my loving Creator saw something in me, something worthy enough to carry the burden of cancer. Through that burden, He began to teach me things about myself and began to grow a relationship with me that can never be broken. I can honestly say that cancer is possibly the best thing that ever happened to me. It made me grow in my spirit, thoughts, and overall perspective on this life I was so graciously given.

My journey with cancer lasted seven years. The beginning phase took me through two and a half years of surgeries and treatments and the remaining five years going back and forth to Houston every six months and then down to once a year for scans and check-ups. My body has beautiful scars that I would not trade for anything, and I have a head full of white hair. I have often referred to my white hair as my "Moses experience" hair. I felt like God had shown me His *glory*! (Exodus 33:18). I also have a lifetime to share God's goodness with people.

# 12

# BEHOLD THE MOTH!

What? You were expecting a butterfly?

Like I said from the beginning, God gave me the title for this book from my MRI tunnel "cocoon." It has been in the process for many years. As I began to write, I was soon reminded of a time much later down the road as my final appointment at MD Anderson approached. It would be my last trip to Houston before a celebratory release from my surgeon, as I knew my scans would be just fine.

I began to reflect on all that I had been able to do with God's help through this process and just how precious those regular life experiences became. I made a top ten list of my life experiences of those last seven years.

You see, my baby was then six years old, and my other children were ages eight, fourteen, and nineteen. I must say I cried as I wrote it because I began to realize that the guilt I felt when I was sick had melted away. I quickly found that my children were thriving, my marriage was strong, and God just poured out blessing after blessing on my family.

Here is the list:

**Top Ten Highlights of the Last Seven Years**

10. I became a published author of my first children's book.

9. I was nominated Teacher of the Year by my colleagues at Wilson Elementary.

8. I saw my oldest son (Wyatt) hit his first home run for his High School baseball team!

7. I taught my younger sons all the things "real kids" need to know: how to tie shoes, blow bubbles with

gum, whistle, and swing in a swing by themselves. More recently, Max learned to ride his bike.

6. I helped my parents maintain their house and take care of them as they got older.

5. I taught students with learning and emotional difficulties how to read and write and gain self-confidence in their abilities.

4. I watched Ethan (who was two) and Max (the baby I was pregnant with when my cancer journey began) start school.

3. I watched my daughter be able to achieve her dreams of attending the college of her choice on an athletic and academic scholarship (Maintain Dean's Honor Roll).

2. I celebrated twenty years of marriage with the love of my life.

1. I learned to be more appreciative, patient, loving, and caring for others and myself too!

I shared this list with friends, family, and coworkers. I must say I had some new coworkers that never knew what I had gone through, but my letter and list touched their lives in a profound way. It made us all think a little deeper about life and the people we share it with. It also gave me a platform to pray with people that I never would have had otherwise or been bold enough to be available to do that. It was quite obvious the experience of cancer had changed me and brought me closer to God.

Just a few months later, a storm had come through our town, and I had gone outside on the morning after, just to see if we had any damage to our house or trees. I did not see any damage, just a few leaves and limbs, but as I turned to go inside, I noticed perched on the bottom panel of my garage door was a huge luna moth with its wings spread wide. I was quite mesmerized by it. It was somewhat understated with its light green color, but it seemed to glow against the white door. It had such a unique shape and creative markings. It was almost like it had been drawn on with a marker.

I had lived in Oklahoma all my life and had never seen one in real life. I called to my children to come look at it, and we all just looked on it in amazement for a little while, then went on about our business. I, for some reason, could not get it off of my mind, and I went back out to look at it. I guess I had some relatable compassion for it, and I wanted to make sure it was alright. It stayed still there until its wings dried, and then it flew off perfectly fine and possibly better than ever.

As I was looking at it, a still, small voice that I know very well chimed up in my spirit. He said, "That's you!" I was a bit puzzled, but the answer came quick, "You have been through the darkness and the storm. You are no longer afraid. You now know how to trust Me and to navigate by the light of My truth. I made you majestically resilient and magnetically hopeful! No longer will you hide!"

Whoa, whoa, whoa! I was speechless, and I just had to write that down. All this time, I thought I was turning into a butterfly, but I was pretty sure the Creator of the universe just told me I was a moth. I was totally surprised that day, and I was totally okay with being a beautiful, relatable, understated moth.

"Therefore if anyone is in Christ, the new creation has come: The old has gone, the new is here!" (2 Corinthians 5:17).

"Forget the former things; do not dwell on the past. See, I am doing a new thing! Now it springs up; do you not perceive it? I am making a way in the wilderness and streams in the wasteland" (Isaiah 43:18-19).

Majestically resilient...I had to think on it a bit. I had been through the wringer in my body, in my thoughts, in my spirit; I even shook my fist at God once or twice. I came out stronger in all of those areas. I tell my story, and people cannot believe that I am healthy. I have peace and a good sense of humor and joy! For the rest of my life, I will be called a *survivor*.

Magnetically hopeful...I have been told I can find the good in almost all situations. You see, my perspective on life is now higher than it once was. I know God's ways are not my ways, but I know that He is working all things for my good. I know people like my smile and my friendly attitude. I am happy to celebrate the life I have been given, the people around me, and the splendor of God's creation!

Navigating by the light of His truth...yep! I have had to learn what God's word says about how to live the right way. I have had to shake off some habits and attitudes that hinder me. I know when the rubber meets the road, God's word stands tested and true. His guidelines are not to bind me up but to show me a better, healthier way to navigate in this world that would have us believe so many lies.

I am fully aware this word is not just for me. It is for every person who has called on the name of Jesus in the face of overwhelming obstacles. This word is for all those who press through and do not give up but let their faith grow in difficulties. This is for all the believers who undoubtedly have no explanation for their healing, peace, strength, and joy but the goodness of God. This word is for people who boldly share their faith with the world.

Originally, I believed that I was not valuable, that my voice did not matter, and that I was insignificant in the grand scheme of this world. I was not important enough for God to care about what I was going through. My cocoon experience made me draw closer and dig into His words. It made me seek the truth about God. It truly built my faith from the ground up. I learned that not everybody gets to know God like I do, but I hope they do! He has shown me how to slow down, to reflect on all the many blessings He has given to me each and every day, to seek the good around me, to obey His commands, to love people, and to encourage them on their perilous journeys.

This is why I choose to lead and attend small groups in my own church. My voice and my actions are important to show how to treat our humanity with the fragile yet awesome reverence it deserves as God's masterpieces. My thoughts are important as they are uniquely mine, breathed to me by the Creator Himself. There is no one like my God, and He created no one else like me. I am thankful He has placed so many precious people, much better than myself, to lead and encourage me.

Another lie is that I had no authority in these life situations when in reality, I have a supreme authority through the work that Jesus did on the cross. I study God's words and His promises. I stand on them and pray them over myself, my family, and friends. I believe it is important for me to pray for people when I see the need or if pressing feelings occur because others need to see and feel the power available to them to overcome illness and obstacles.

I have a spirit of love, of power, and a sound mind. I have made up my mind to trust the Lord with all of my heart (Proverbs 3:5). With that being said, I want everything in my life to point the way to a loving, comforting, healing Jesus and a mountain-moving God!

I am fully aware that I am not perfect, and God is not finished working on me, as our human metamorphosis is like no other. It is a constant cycle. Some lessons may have a longer process, and I am open to the fact that if at any time He needs to show me something new about myself, life, my relationship with Him, or anything else I need to be educated on, He may choose to pull me back in that cocoon and create something different. For now, I will be happy with who He made me to be, a most grateful and humble moth!

"Do not conform to the pattern of this world, but be transformed by the renewing of your mind. Then you will be able to test and approve what God's will is his good, pleasing and perfect will" (Romans 12:1-2).

CPSIA information can be obtained
at www.ICGtesting.com
Printed in the USA
BVHW051517051021
618203BV00007B/254